To say I have a wide selection of umbilical cords and dried foreskins hanging from my ceiling would be a lie. What an interesting concept though. I think I'd paint them bright colors. I do collect banana peels, dry them, paint them various colors and hang them from my rather large ears. Always gets a comment at parties.

W ell friends, this is number eighteen in a series of chapbooks I'm happy to be able to present to you through Grayhair Press. Everyone at Grayhair Press is required to hang painted banana peels from their ears. It's like a contest, seeing who can come up with the most original fruity art.

I don't know about you guys but sometimes I feel fruity and sometimes I feel totally straight. Never did come out of any closet or have desire to make any sexual statements. I guess I'm selfish as I love vaginas and penis's but can't stand all the bullshit that comes along with them. You know, egos and personalities. I guess I'm a glory hole person.

Anyway, I hope you'll like this collection. My desire is to win the Pulitzer Prize for Poetry before I die. Better hurry Brownie...you're seventy and failing fast. Peace to you all.

Dick

CHAPBOOKS BY DICK BROWN

EATING THE LIGHT

SEA OF JAPAN

HOUSE OF SPARROWS

KENOSHA POEMS

THE OHIO OF THE MOON

BROKEN ARROW NOCTURNE

BREAKING AND ENTERING

NEW AND SELECTED POEMS

ELEVEN DOMESTIC POEMS

POEMS FOR TRANNIES

BECOMING INVISIBLE

WINTER POEMS 2004

THIS MINDS BLOOD

UNSOLICITED MANUSCRIPTS

SALAD MANIA

MORNING RUSH

WHAT KIND OF TREE IS HAPPENING

WITHERING MANOR

Published in the United States of America by
Grayhair Press.®

Grayhair Press ® and colophon are the property

of Grayhair Press.®

Library of Congress Cataloging-in-Publication Data

Brown, Richard.

Poems for Trannies / Dick Brown

ISBN 978-0-9843260-2-0

Printed in the United States of America

First Printing

Book Design…..Dixie Collette

詩

POEMS

FOR

TRANNIES

SITTING UNDER A WALNUT TREE
IN LAFORTUNE PARK, TULSA, OKLAHOMA
The cold aristocrats that die
Left you alone in your defeat.
                    --James A. Wright

Green fire of black walnut undulate

on September Oklahoma afternoon.

Nearby, a shiny, red Wheel Horse

is noisily chasing its tail like a kitten.

Deeper into the Saturday afternoon

a distant steeple with weathervane

hovers above the hydrangea bushes

shaking their clenched petaline fists.

Here on a dry trip from the dry out

facility where fools like me end up

(when lucky enough to get this far)

I sit with rotten teeth and long hair

under a walnut tree on an old earth

angry that I've run out of cigarettes.

To the *gallinas* of the hallways

where I write and rest my head:

your minding your business business

is running in the red.

DRIVING KAHZ

You stop your breathing to listen
but you can hear another breathing
and conclude that there are two,
two of you living here:
the breathing you recognize
and the mystical phantom wheezing.
Your phantom king is Emphysematous,
Lord of Lungia and North Susperia;
he expectorants your subservience.
What of your anxiety disorders?
You're hesitant to meet anyone.
And to make matters absurd,
the queens drank in the bahs
of Lawrence and New Bedford
with the smack and toot gods.

A CROSSDRESSER DREAMS HIS AURA
A land of dreams I roam.
--John G. Whittier

His cat creeps to the looking glass
but does not see her reflection.
Sans ego, her mirror is a window
through which she looks outside:
chipmunks scurry over gray stones,
birds search for food, a field mouse.

Oh, if he could only visit there,
inward to the pith of creation
and the myriaplanets living there.
He would sail into oblivious orbits
sans ennui during the journey
to guaranteed safe landing sites.

Somewhere, near the largest crater
he'd swish about in lacey underalls
beside the number two rocket stand.

EAST HAVERHILL STREET

I'm sitting on a curbstone of my seventieth year.
Been here since the sixties or seventies and my
boney ass is getting sore. Same cars passing by,
same beautifully-faced, fine tits and ass women,
time pleading amnesia, my drugs my tabula rasa.
After watching it all this time I have it down pat.
It'll turn left on Park at the end of East Haverhill
and as soon as it goes out of sight she'll walk by,
the gal from Newbury Street with long black hair,
the chick I loved even though my wife was there.
That particular wife divorced me many years ago.
Mary was a plain-clothed cunt loaded with morals
who dumped me for dealing heroin and infidelity,
for cutting them both with lactose and Epsom salts,
one for the rent and the other for the wicked rush.

THIS MIND'S BLOOD
Lake Attitash, Merrimac, MA

It was summer, the rainfall,

August drizzle falling to fill

the aquifers and jellymelons

was blowing off to Amesbury.

Through after-rain gray mist,

the reddish sun, pinker of hills,

stainer of the ruddy filament,

pinked this mind's blood.

Imagine a pink-stained cloud

penciled in the rain moment.

"Just walk along and ignore it,"

mother would always caution,

"don't speak to anything pink."

A VOICE FOR RAINY DAYS
cogito, ergo sum
--Descartes

He hadn't slept with rhyming
since going to bed with Oklahoma,
she learned him that souls
could also be found on boots.

He could never return
to the same state twice
unless butterfly moments
bounced along the tip of his net
black and purple thigh-highs.

He had some trouble
hanging in there with the tenses
sometimes feeling guilty for being alive.

A strong young man, with a ponytail,
just rode over and scalped his grave.

Mimosa vacillates above
the throbbing goldenrod.
Where are you going he giggles?

At Garabedian's farm
they taught us how
to bleach celery.

MIRROR AGAINST TREE
AT ROADSIDE DUMP

I spit into the face of Time
That has transfigured me.

--W. B. Yeats

Ordinarily he wouldn't look

but today he's reminiscing

of how handsome he used to be,

wants to know what happened.

He delves into the reflection,

stares intently at the eyes:

they are the hazel of his youth,

but his smile shows rotted teeth.

He demands audience with his ogre,

begs it to step out and touch him,

soothe him, speak of youthful times.

He shuffles the attitude of the glass,

but the incidence and reflection

are preoccupied with themselves

and supine on the quicksilver.

They have become schizophrenic,

inured to the fantasies of old creamers.

OKMULGEE LOTION

Just inside my pouting, painted lips
tiny lavender and orange butterflies
peek out at me as I beautify my face.
I wonder if they'll emerge, fluttering,
as I begin spinning my lipstick shut,
will they see Rorschachs hunting the
hamadryad virgins in chestnut trees?
I read once in the Hamadryad Journal
that pure or emphysematous lungs
can breathe as easily as wall aliens
bracing their legs for orgasms.

from the *Goddess of Hope* series

TUMBLING

I've be tumbling along

longer than most tumble.

It's saddening, but I guess

it's kinda like when it's time

to tumble you bloody tumble.

My mother was a tumbler

from South New Bedford.

She vodka'd and cigaretted

for the better part of 1940

for sex partners to entumble

her blonde, little dumb bard.

Tumblers sailed on her ocean.

I think I take after the one

who after landing at Normandy

tumbled immediately onto the sand

and was posthumously made a kernel.

--tr. from p380 (Peono)
Collected Works of Sdaehtihs
by Dick Brown

CUNNILINGUS

Sleep-depraved and miserable
there's no escape with drugs
and alcohol doze any more
as I'm too old, hung sickly
and lackluster at napping.
The poet, Gaylord Farquar
Guadalajaras at such times.
I don't have enough money
to possibly Guadalajara
but can imagine Kenosha Creek:
laying on the declivities there
watching naked stones and water
rush by on well formed, naked legs.
I'm tired of holding up my sperm.

BLUSTER IN TULSA

A chill no coat, however stout,
Of homespun stuff could quite
shut out...
--John Greenleaf Whittier

The wind direction shifts

and it becomes apparent

that Tulsa's blowing asunder.

The weather guru, Giles,

opens his coat for kids

as piles of water freeze

and begin to back up like

corpses in Port au Prince.

Today, storms blow in like

Olympian weather gods:

two category five Islamic

tornados run along East 71st street

thumping their Korans

with C-4 hid in their diapers.

GINSBERG IN OKLAHOMA

Most words are uttered
for the sake of rhyme
and not for an image
like a mosquito buzzing
in and out the interstices
of coquettish lily pads.

Wise old deck hands
stagger through opium
and with soft voices
create smoky poetry.

The New York Jews
are shaking their fists.
Mr. Alan Ginsberg
uttered the word "fuck"
several times
during a poetry reading
at Oklahoma University.
I reek of bald cypress and semen.

RUBYTHROAT

On September 27th, 2009
our hummingbirds
departed for El Salvador.
We couldn't help notice
that the tiny one
who flew with his legs
held in a funny position
and had been showing up
for the past few years
never showed in 2009.
I guess they only live a short time.
Funny how we can remember
such small details about birds
and know nothing of cancer.

SIXTY ONE WEBSTER

…this overmade world
where old paths are submerged
in metal and cement.
--Jim Harrison

I've recently returned from New England

where I visited the commune I grew up on

and attended my fiftieth high school reunion.

My daughter, Lynn Ann, drove us around

Andover, Hampton, Salisbury, Plum Island,

Lawrence and the Salem of New Hampshire.

We devoured fried clams and haddock filets.

The house dad built at Sixty One Webster St.

had been assimilated by the concrete gods.

We had a tasty sandwich called a *Steak Bomb*

before visiting the cemetery where I used to work.

At the cemetery, I thought of Oklahoma;

not that I wasn't enjoying New England,

but no one had trimmed around the stones.

My old friend Sexuality
rests supine on the couch
in her usual position.

C.O.P.D.

Heavy with cigarette smoke for fifty five years I am having trouble breathing these days. I don't know how much longer I have on this Earth for as I get older it becomes more of a task to keep the spark glowing. I wonder, if I should be so lucky as to go to Heaven, if there is such a venue, if they allow smoking there? And what if one contracts COPD in Heaven…where does one go from there. Do you think God smokes? Does he smoke Camels? Does he carry an oxygen bottle around, possibly attached to his wheelchair or does he use a walker. Does he, oh, excuse me…maybe God's an old woman. Did God hang around out in the hallways of Heaven gossiping about everybody in the place? If I'm lucky enough to get there, if such a place exists, I surely hope I'll be assigned a private room. I'll sit at my heavenly computer all day, if days exist, and write what never came to mind on Earth. I'll also smoke one butt after another all day long…Camels, without a filter.

It's ten o'clock in the morning
and Sky's taking her morning walk
with her white poodle on a leash.

CENOTAPH

More monument than poem
I read the bloody anecdote
below it: "In my museum
I want to see some spirit
sort of standing before it:
a large brush in one hand
a stain can in the other.
A sinewy, red headed,
sleeves rolled to biceps
Abroathen spirit, powerful,
thick-wristed and proud
after I've published the forest
one of my kids might have
in an old paragraph album."

BARKING CONSERVATIVES
for Duffy, Dawnie, Bonnie and Jeanie

Ever begin *your own* path?

I've been beginning for seventy years,

and still have to shield my eyes

from brambles and twiggy snapbacks.

My puberty path in Andover

was paved with morality tiles

stretching to Boutwell's farm.

I celebrate the four collies

sitting off to the right.

Next, my god and kingdoms,

time worn cliché who desires

like liquid in crucible

to be original ejaculate.

The shotgun leaning against the pine

hitchhiked here from North Dakota.

The four collies came in from the heat.

Poetry is one of the positions

we assume

while fucking.

BARN ASIDE TURNPIKE

Somebody poemed

nestlings among

rafters and beams

and an old man

in red-rimmed,

black, knee-high

rubber boots

steel-wheeled wheel barrowing

sweet manure

over wobbly planks

to the brown dune.

Every so often

as they are wont to do

in rural Oklahoma

finches and swallows

shake from the engine

as Muskogee dobbins

shiver their withers

and flail course swishers

at twelve-point font neo-maggots

If I should lose sight privileges
will you read poems
to my grounded pilots?

OLIVIA
for Wilmatine

If I had the choice
I think I'd rather be
in Checotah, Oklahoma
than in the Xanadu of Olivia
without you.

PASQUINADE

A woman strolls into the Peppermint Lounge
and requests that the girl standing by the mic
enquire over the loudspeakers if someone's there:
"Is Mike Hunt out there?" the mic girl blares
over a system cranked up for beach club music.
"Someone's looking for Mike Hunt." she yells.
I chuckle that it could be Mike Hunt's old lady
out checking bars to maybe catch him cheating;
maybe grinding cheek to cheek with that bird
he's been secretly meeting up with for strange.
Mike Hunt never did come forward that night.
He sat quietly in a far corner deeply engrossed,
smoking cigarette after cigarette--passionately
composing a pasquinade for the shithouse wall.

ALL THOSE SEASONS

If you'd listened carefully
on windy summer days
you'd have heard the leaves.
It's autumn now, old fag
and your lawn is littered
with entertainers like them
who sang their hearts out for you.
Always too self-absorbed,
you never heard their music.
It's taken all these seasons
just to realize how deaf you have been
and now, Dixie, you deliquesce.

I studied Latin in college
but graduated
barely understanding
my English boyfriend.

Let me be remembered

as the erection

that lasted more than four hours.

Sometimes I wake up
in the middle of a climax
cumming and going.

In order to be accepted

mediocrity

must be fresh and original.

MORNING RUSH
for Bob Eichling

It's seven A.M.—oh-- dear God--
they've overslept, they'll lose their job!
The big boss told them yesterday
that when they're late he'll dock their pay
and if they're late too many times
they'll be included for their crimes
in unemployment's swelling lines.

They've many innocents to kill:
woodchuck, squirrel, whippoorwill
that cross their egocentric ride
and never reach the other side.
Butcher squirrel, slaughter cat,
disembowel the school-bound brat
and leave it there, run over flat.

At night--it's not as bad,
they're exhausted, not as mad
as in the morning rush to punch the clock,
one shoe tied, one brown--one charcoal sock.
Punch in at eight, out at end of day;
kill anything to get that goddam pay;
killed our cocker spaniel yesterday.

SAFETY KIT

We climaxed

and after she fell asleep,

I pulled on my jumper and 13 buttons,

picked up my shoes and tiptoed

out of the Viasalgia Hotel

and into a New York City dawn.

I hailed a cab outside the lobby.

"Get a safety kit," the cabbie said.

"I'll stop by a druggist so you can."

What's a safety kit I asked?

"It's a little tube of cream

you squeeze into the hole in the head.

It'll make anything you might have

picked up in New York City go away."

A red wasp

sips dewdrops

from a dark green glass.

The puppy, Bandit,
on one of his early sojourns
decided to make us
his home base.
One day he wandered
down to Route 62.
We're not sure if
he chased cars there
or the neighbor's weenie.
We'll remember him
as the cute little mutt
who was carefree
and got smitten
by a Firestone.

lost in spindrift

one morning
i saw it walking the beach
kicking dry seaweed

i yelled good morning
but it didn't stop
it kept walking and kicking

oh to be sea detritus
Atlantic integument
entangled there

one morning i saw it
kicking dry seaweed
like it didn't give a shit.

BALL AT WITCH CITY

Our partners in black

in keeping with the trend

toward occultisizing America

have daubed amitriptyline

on their wrists and earlobes.

They wear Blavatsky teeshirts.

They've become wildflowers

at the Salem Wiccan Ball,

root-dancing

along a shady lane

between Barack Obama

and the Black Sabbath tune

about electric pollination.

If they fall, they can't get up.

You can see their nipples.

Lately on television
we're threatened with heart ailments,
acid reflux disease,
four hour erections,
chronic dry eye,
restless leg syndrome
and every conceivable form of cancer.
I'll take the four hour erections.

THE T/V
MEDICINE SHOW

For just and only

special price + tax,

a limited time only.

Save, Just and Only

are warning signs.

Wake up, America,

marketers are liars,

cheats and deceivers.

Read their fine print

if you can even see it.

Participation required.

caveat emptor

American consumer,

gullible, oh so gullible.

MEMOIRS OF A DRAG QUEEN

She's a lonely, old queen
named Dixie Arthritis.
Born in an abandoned
horseshoe crab shell
in sea cock harbor muck
at New Bedford, Massachusetts.
She had difficulty
with the self-righteous Baptists
in Oklahoma.
Her amphetamine heart
backed up from the soul's brain
on a hillside in Muskogee.
She could hear raidos coming up the hill
so she hunched down and pretended she wasn't.

Once, in Oklahoma,
we saw sunlight bouncing
off the nose of an echo.